T0355239

Tractor and Digger

Karra McFarlane

OXFORD
UNIVERSITY PRESS

OXFORD
UNIVERSITY PRESS

Great Clarendon Street, Oxford, OX2 6DP, United Kingdom

Oxford University Press is a department of the University of Oxford. It furthers the University's objective of excellence in research, scholarship, and education by publishing worldwide. Oxford is a registered trade mark of Oxford University Press in the UK and in certain other countries

Text © Karra McFarlane 2016

Illustrations © Michelle Ouellette 2016

Inside cover notes written by Catherine Baker

The moral rights of the author have been asserted

First published 2016

British Library Cataloguing in Publication Data
Data available

ISBN: 978-0-19-837079-6

11

Paper used in the production of this book is a natural, recyclable product made from wood grown in sustainable forests. The manufacturing process conforms to the environmental regulations of the country of origin.

Printed in China by Shanghai Offset Printing Products Ltd

Acknowledgements

Series Editor: Nikki Gamble

The publisher would like to thank the following for permission to reproduce photographs:

Cover and p11: Verena Matthew/Dreamstime; **Back Cover:** SeDmi/Shutterstock; **p2 and p12e**: Natbar/Istockphoto; **p3 and p12a**: Ltroky/Alamy; **p4**: Ana de Castillo/Shutterstock; **p5 and p12f**: Chris Laurens/Getty Images; **p6b**: Air Images/Shutterstock; **p6t and p12b**: Tanja Mjatov/Shutterstock; **p7**: geogphotos/Alamy; **p8l**: Ian Lishman/Juice Images/Corbis; **p8r and P12c**: Izzy71/Shutterstock; **p9b**: smileymikey1/Shutterstock; **p9t and p12h**: SeDml/Shutterstock; **p10 and p12d and p12i**: Fotokostic/Shutterstock; **p12g**: Anon Pichit/Istockphoto.

bucket

cab

Contents

cab

5

seeds

I can put in the seeds.

crops

I am the best!
I can pick up
the grain.

grain

I can dig the track.

I can go on the track.

Tractor and Digger

seeds

 mud

 crops

ditch

 grain

track

track